MINARETS

ISSUE TWO, SPRING

A POETRY JOURNAL

EDITED BY
CHRIS HOLDAWAY & LAUREN STRAIN

BELL TOWER PRESS
2012

Published in New Zealand in 2012
by Bell Tower Press
minaretsjournal.com

Cover design by Chris Corson-Scott
Printed in the United States of America

ISSN 047322805X
ISBN 978-0-473-22805-7

Thanks to

James Wylie & Sam Thomas
Tessa Stubbing

CONTENTS

INTRODUCTION

The number of self-published periodicals that begin with best intentions yet never make it to a second edition could fill an ocean... or perhaps a large lake. Following the debut-issue elation, we experienced the inertia and faced the realisation that we had to do it all again. We learned much from last time, have hopefully grown as editors, and believe that we are now able to offer an even more comprehensive issue.

There have been changes. While previously we solicited work from familiar poets, this time around we opened the doors to submissions. We received brilliant pieces that we would not have otherwise come across, broadening our reach to various areas of New Zealand. These pieces come from diverse sources, including creative writing schools such as the International Institute of Modern Letters at the Victoria University of Wellington; artists active in other mediums, including music and film; and poets working outside traditional institutions.

Spring, 2012 is a mixture of these exciting discoveries along with pieces from several poets who were invited to share their wonderful words. There are some names returning from the previous issue, and we are proud to once again showcase two international writers whose work would otherwise be unlikely to reach our shores. Wary of catering only to young 'twenty-something' upstarts, we are also very pleased to feature some more established, 'mature' poets. Naturally, these developments have seen the publication grow in physical size.

We hope readers will share our enthusiasm for this collection.

Since the release of the *Winter, 2012* issue at the beginning of August, *Minarets* has enjoyed a number of successes, including Auckland Zinefest, and a launch event at Snake Pit Gallery in Auckland. Contributors attending gave striking readings, while the work of those overseas or in other parts of the country was displayed in large-scale print on the gallery walls. Our first issue continues to retail online at Amazon.com, and in paper at Time Out Bookstore in Auckland. We will also be on the road next month for Wellington Zinefest.

So far we've made good on our quarterly promise. Wish us continued luck.

Chris Holdaway
Lauren Strain
Editors
October, 2012
Auckland, NZ

MINARETS

ISSUE TWO / SPRING 2012

ZARAH
BUTCHER-McGUNNIGLE

Wellington, NZ

1

We were going to. After switching damaging recover. (we need more pronouns.) Grass aches against the epicentre of baldness. Since, may, continuous, concede. (Mother. Move your hair. The bald spot is showing.) To abnormalise: (Describe the worst event in your childhood.) To thaw pre-frozen emotion: (Imagine you've just won a prize. What do your parents say.)

2

"No" lacks a bloodstream, she forgets it can be a complete sentence. A part and apart. Come to dinner, we're having the skulls of mushrooms. (But there's no room for me.) Socialise, generalise, compromise, improvise, circumcise, no surely not. Appetiser: what do you do, I mean for a living, no, what do you really do. (But I don't take up any room.) My blood is too loud, I can't think. (Dinner parties are not parties. Parties are not parties either.) She takes the long way home. (I'm sorry, I can't come to dinner tonight, I'm going to get a headache.)

She plays the cello inside a cell (inside a cell). Membrane, member, are you are member of this family or an appendage. Invest, test, best, modest, crest. The child broke. The child broke her wrist. (If it hadn't been for that injury, you'd have been a "star") (If it hadn't been for that injury, I'd have been a "star").

RICHARD OSLER

Duncan, B.C., Canada

Going to Church In Nyamata, Rwanda

Let the tin roof creak and groan.
There are no sounds but this.
Small sounds.
The sound the sun becomes
on a hot tin roof.

These corrugations perfectly straight
high above the tiled crypt,
catacomb and skulls, thousands,
mirthless, having a last laugh.

Dust combs through cavities for secrets written in invisible
    ink.
I want distance, measurements.
By the foot, by the inch.
By the inch, a world

moves closer.

Clutch a rosary. No bridge
between here
and a puzzled god.

After Seventy Years

Her kisses are missing. Call 911. My mother,
her eyes, are missing, their colour, blue,
Precambrian lake blue, that old, that used
to a world, in its spin, its rounds around
a necessary brightness. The sun is missing.
The purple flowers of the Agapanthus lily
are missing. Gone seventy years. My mother
is lost. Call 911. She wanders from room to room,
passes through my father, leaves parts of herself,
like smoke from her Buckingham's. It gathers
inside him, holds a blackness from buried years,
layer by layer – pressure and heat. My mother
is listening in a chair, in a room, to an agapanthus
that she wanted after my grandmother cared for it
for seventy years without a bloom. My mother
is missing. Call 911. She's lost in a dream,
a lily asleep in the arms of the first purple bloom.

EDEN BRADFIELD

Oamaru, NZ

Sandra, 41

the back of her van says 'exotic plants' but i am not so sure
if there's many plants in there at all because when i saw
her husband – let's call him glen – unload a box, beige and
unfussy,
(he wore khaki shorts and a plaid shirt himself)
i did not see any exotic plants

she herself – we'll call her sandra, pronounced
SAN-dra, not SEN-dra or SAND-ra
(she's very particular about this sort of thing)
has a shock blonde hairdo like she spun her hair too many
    times
in the candyfloss maker
and wears leopard print blouses
– pretty exotic if you ask me

yet between the two of them and their van
(which has a palm tree on the back, i might add)
i have seen not an iota of an exotic plant in sight

KATIE WINNY

Auckland, NZ

self-timer

Subject matter: self, at a teetering age.
Self, in skinny furs, enamel brooch slipping off
sagging blouse, an avalanche. Self asks self,
are you okay. There is no need to be.
Harnessed clutch of hair, trailing over shoulder
as a bundled animal. Self is ruptured open
by the cold. Confused lambs die in the dark,
petrified in snow. Little stiff blankets,
the next day they are piled high.

Analysis of a dream: self struggles
to suppress your ghost.

vinzel

September glimpsed
through the open back of my black dress
unbuttoned, strung up
by a single wire hanger

the homemade abortionists' kind

there's noise through the balcony doors
city cars, in country lanes
passing the pregnant vines

with their fat roe clustered
in the lower branches,

I've seen nothing yet
for such a deflowered traveller
my clothes still smelling of Rome
the sweet damp dust, on everything
and my suitcase life

spread out on another foreign floor

I catch French
conversation
car starts up and leaves the drive
with places to go, out of my life
much the same as I

left time and again
breath held and eyes slow
through a plane window,
at each city's lights

rested on their black beds

all my mythology shattered
about otherness and distance,
because even you
are still in the world.

MARK PIRIE

Wellington, NZ

School's Out

Autumn leaves; ain't no
summer up here, I'm crawling
along the roof
                    school's out
and so are the lights.

Not much of a weekend –
usual entertainment: a DVD
a game and a piss-up;
                    instead I'm
up here. The night-chill
stiffens my cheek. I prise off
the copper right beside
the High Voltage
                    power line.

I make it, just, and inch back
towards the others. They're
working on the middle block.
I used to go here once, so I
                    know my
way round the sheds and backs
of the houses, know where to go if
we need to escape…

*Hurry, pigs'll be here
soon!* someone says. A neighbour's
lights go on up the hill. I topple
down with my loot, and wait to
scram.
              We did good,
a man says as the youngest of
us falls with a spark and a crackle
and a loud thump to the ground.

MEGAN TOWEY

Annandale-on-Hudson, NY, USA

World of Floods

Driving on the curb cured of swamplands and horizontals
my atmosphere dear takes wholesome bites of water
outed are the undersides of bridge smudged chasms
birdy hellcalls and undone song
he knows only fire pursues the winged
torn letters three years gone of the antediluvian
disintegrated into charm and clarity and the promise
of a moment in time that springs everlastingly
will be flooded

and the pulmonary one ways dripping varied shades of
    moving cars
in fresh killed greys keeping time with the hacks of self
    against love
while our hands are crossed in universes pleading
with the dying that cannot slow down but winds and winds
    around
the pulsed city of language tying the sacred grammar to
    plurals
another and another
until they grow into the flicking tongue that time will
    harness
to toss rogue prophets into the pockets of New Jersey
where in being shelved we meet among starships
will be flooded

and the candles that when burning exhale signatures into
    the air
distinct enough to merge
into the piney and nuclear silhouette of one jacket hung on
    two shoulders
strong enough to fold the page
of the cosmic fairytale of a lonely planet spinning gone
blue enough to germinate
the thousand seeded blanknesses that for a sacred miracle
    have
ego enough to tumble down
and resting softly on the lower back of some sweet
    polygonal
concave enough to hold them
come to agree on one straight line of thought both concise
    and
true enough to love forever
will be flooded

Heartmind

We lost electricity on the night you left me
and I spent the night curled up against the rain,
drinking in the slack of damp green winds
in our treasured driftwood home of mist.
I had to come to think of time
as a medium and my thoughts as
imperfect and cursive. It was a wrinkled medium,
a mediocrity of sunken breath: words condensing
into droplets that so contorted my teary lenses
that I couldn't tell that you were turning towards me

with a sound, the sound a book makes
when its leaves are rustled against the grain.
Tonight my body lingers on the edge of the ocean
like a gasp; New Jersey's throaty highways
bear my rosefelt thoughts and I can't miss them
like I miss the cradle of the river,
like I miss the firm grip of the circular,
like I miss the existential faith we had in nature
and her artistic lover to take us home.

CAMERON CHURCHILL

Auckland, NZ

Holes

I am the man who
digs a trench, four walls for you
walls made of mud
four eyes made for the cathedral
how pretty it would be to be with a beauty in the country
but here I am with the worms in the mud

I can smell excess
this hellhole reeks of excess
of worms gorged on garbage
it's on my cold hands, mud covered
every coffee cup from here to kansas
emptied on the surface and sunk down, settled in

The beauty in my mind is now laying on the beach
her hands are on her hips and my tongue is in her teeth
and the light from the hotel behind her silhouettes her
    shape to me
I sigh and stub my cigarette, her head turns up to me
hm, my imagination's cheesy
Like bad film noir

The bombers blaze ahead
above my hole in the night sky
1943, the cities of Europe are up in flames

and the only thing to blame is a few mad imaginations
including my own damn imagination
as I sit and think of WWIII and grant the thought reality

Everyday begins with coffee and digging
and everyday ends with the closing of blinds
the beauty holds on tight, in the hole in my mind
the hole of the whole in this hellhole at night

Doctor

"Kill me" my doctor said, I have the worst doctor in the
    world

My Doctor keeps calling me at night reminding me I could
    die any minute

I told my doctor that I went to another doctor who said I
    DON'T have lymphoma
my doctor was mad that I cheated on him, I am mad
    because he intentionally pretended I had lymphoma
our relationship is not very healthy at the moment

My doctor is from Somalia, his dad is a pirate
who ever heard of a Somalian Doctor?
I think maybe my doctor is just a pirate in disguise

My Doctor told me my feet were "gross"

My doctor uses words like "illin', buzzy, brosef, bitch,
    cracker"

My doctor is always bragging about how much weed he
    can smoke

LYNLEY EDMEADES

Dunedin, NZ

La Strada

Roads are never busy here – the further
south you go, the less narrative you see.
It's autumn – going south means gold.
A gold that will soon turn to just tree.

I stop to visit an old friend, her new baby.
Another place, a new couple – I drink wine
and relish in their getting-to-each-other bliss;
Too much of both, not enough of this.

Next town, a poet friend – he's coming down
off an acid bender, and I'm wearing
the wrong shoes. We find a quiet place to talk
about form, structure, Wellington, Dunedin.

I hear myself saying hello goodbye soon
keep in touch take care of course you too.
I'm headed for my own – a space
to gather dust in, spread myself, like glue.

Terminus

I left you there in June, watched
you cycle away with the morning,
the road behind you turning to dust
under an incessant Apollo.
Your house was a kind of terminus,
and its portico, the platform.

I watched your mother taking trips
to the garden and hanging washing.
She spoke to me of weeds, the heat,
how she'd once thought she too might travel.
No question now of her whereabouts,
I thought, as I posed static

and balconied, in the infinite potential
of being away from my own life.
Yes, I thought, I could stay here,
let the days work away, decided.
While I'm thinking this, there's a knock
at the door – *mi scusi, la pasta è pronta*.

MAGNOLIA WILSON

Wellington, NZ

National Anxiety

The party is very loud and mostly the view is just of a
    hundred pairs
of highly glittered or neon shoes, wide angled along a
    gummy hardwood floor.

So much coloured and stomping and endless stomping.

Late in the night, when bodies finally hang like deflated
    Lilos over couches,
you, in someone else's room where the walls are only dirty
    white sheets,
have rough sex with Richie McCaw.

He is much more aggressive than you'd imagined. His TV
    persona –
a giant jelly-baby implanted with a 'sporting platitudes'
    chip,
isn't quite as *sweet as* …

A short time after ripping off your black undies and going
    down, he
surfaces, furiously, to inform you that your Brazilian isn't
    up to par …

you might want to rethink your strategy, work on your
    game, if you
know what he means, for the national good, of course.

ALEX TAYLOR

Auckland, NZ

close[t/d]

you're determined that nobody
knows what you're really like
how you actually are what
planet you're from it's
difficult to construct an
impression when you do it
so badly

perhaps that's why nobody
mistakes you for yourself
I never would have picked you
as if that is
a kind of compliment

you wonder if you ever learned
to take such a thing –
praise, criticism, a sharp look,
a tender squeeze

for a while you decide you'll
transcribe everything he says
so you'll learn to take it
it's more objective that way it
doesn't fester in your head

after a while you feel
different somehow
the slope of your moods is
gentler you're able to express
more complex ideas your
skin more and more is
reminiscent of windows

park bench

he said he didn't think
you would've come
and you didn't either

but now you have
and your double entendre
has deserted you

outside, a cold day

having to arrive early you have time
to forget what s/he looks like your
free ticket the sound of caster sugar

the leaks in your memory are
riveting you renegade the sky
your old gossip spills out you're
not you won't you wouldn't have

the clouds open behind you

LAUREN STRAIN

Auckland, NZ

Years

and so much life – years full as the sky
in a Dark August. I wish that words
could rain from my hands too, but they never come out.

But my sister is more beautiful; she is the yellow room
Set against thundery skies. Even when we were small,
She was Snow White to my Rose Red.

She is running down a road, spinning pirouettes,
skilled in the sorcery of our mothers. Even as the seasons
    fall,
lit leaves in a smoky wood,

she holds out her hand to me.
Does she know I love her, but I am hopeless
at growing straight, like a beanstalk? Because I am learning
    slowly

that our building blocks, our puzzle pieces
click together in mechanical harmony, are a
perfect fit despite their asymmetry;

so when we meet, my sister,
your life spun into gold
as I try to stamp you to a page,

all is not as it was, but all is well
(you see, we can no longer be the same
by dressing in stripes) because
photographs are clearer than mirrors
and stormy grey Augusts
suit bright April skies.

Birds

Once, when I was four,
and out with my grandmother, I was
entranced by the birds. They were tiny thumbtacks
stuck to the purple sky, dwarfed by the salty crashes
slapping away the walkway by the beach.

Like a gull pinned against a dark expanse, my grandmother
is a small bird in her bed. Finely boned,
her head nods gently. Her eyes are bright.
My grandfather stands beside her, upright as a heron
    perched on broken edges,
on the rocks curled about the tide.

She is paused mid-flight, but soon she'll rise
in a gentle flurry, like those birds
that only seemed stuck, but glide –
that I'm remembering now in swells and ebbs.

OLIVER QUINCY PAGE

Auckland, NZ

For Evan Blumgart

I've never said anything
that rivals your one pointed breath
the finest thought I've ever known.
You belong in the slipstream
of casual carless love and wanderings
in a city that beats out your name
on worn asphalt
heat rising off a loft roof in waves.
You are afraid, '…edibility of my soul.'
of dorm rooms and academic curses
but you will win at this –
you win brilliantly, in earnest –
gift new light to the firmament.
Emery Roth steel runs crack
but we know the dead will walk again
on film – at the movies
second run picture houses.
You will wander into the cinema
drag on the mood lighting
all cool – auburn
bruised ego, doughy and
dishevelled and the most
compelling facial hair this side of
Henry Wadsworth Longfellow.

You will find a language
of private signs and notations
of shared experiences.
My dearest friend is ageless.

I'm half stolen

I washed your body
methodically – workmanlike
It was a task and I accepted it with all the mood I had in
    me

I shaved your head
some other gesture
I performed with the care of the servants you prayed to

I kissed your eyelids
last in a line of the unhappy few
I want to mean more than all the others

I'd cut my hand, I'd burn my back

I'd daven with you
Real Siddur in hand – whiter knuckles
listening for the lyric and note that set you alight

ידי את רוחץ אני
בעפר מוכתמת הלבנה הפורצלן רצפת
הנקיות מידי צשובות רוצה אני

50

CONTRIBUTORS

Zarah Butcher-McGunnigle has a BA from the University of Auckland, and is currently completing an MA in Creative Writing at Victoria University's IIML. Her work has appeared in publications such as *Sport*, *Turbine*, *Landfall*, *Horse Less Review*, and *Colorado Review*.
Say hello: zarahbm@hotmail.co.nz.

Richard Osler, poet and money manager, lives in Duncan, B.C., Canada. His chapbook of small poems *Where the Water Lives* was published by Leaf Press in 2012. His poems have appeared also in journals including *CV2*, *Malahat Review*, *Antigonish Review*, *Prairie Fire* and *Ruminate Magazine* in the U.S. In 2011 he was shortlisted for the Malahat Open Season Awards in poetry. He also leads poetry workshops in drug and alcohol recovery centres.

Eden Bradfield writes mostly short stories, sometimes longer stories and very occasionally poems. They have previously been published in *Takahe*, *Elle*, and *Pop* magazine, among others.

Katie Winny is studying Film & Media Studies and English at the University of Auckland. She reads between the lines.

Mark Pirie is an internationally published New Zealand poet, editor, and critic. He co-founded *JAAM* (Just Another Art Movement) literary magazine from 1995-2005 in Wellington and currently edits the chapbook journal, *broadsheet: new new zealand poetry*. He is the managing editor/publisher for the small press HeadworX. Many collections of his poetry have appeared (including Gallery, Salt, UK, 2003) and he has edited anthologies, including *The NeXt Wave* (Gen X New Zealand writing, 1998) and *A Tingling Catch: A Century of New Zealand Cricket Poems 1864-2009* (2010). He currently co-organizes the Poetry Archive of New Zealand Aotearoa (PANZA), with Niel Wright and Michael O'Leary.

Megan Towey is an undergraduate at Bard College, where she studies poetry and classical studies. She lives in the Hudson River Valley.

Cameron Churchill (born 31 July 1965), is a British novelist, best known as the author of the Harry Potter fantasy series. The Potter books have gained worldwide attention, won multiple awards, and sold more than 400 million copies. They have become the best-selling book series in history, and the basis for a popular series of films, in which Cameron had overall approval on the scripts as well as maintaining creative control by serving as a producer on the final installment. Cameron conceived the idea for the series on a train trip from Manchester to London in 1990.

Lynley Edmeades is currently based in Dunedin, where she is working on a postgraduate thesis on the poetics of John Cage at the University of Otago. In 2011 she attained an MA with Distinction from the Seamus Heaney Centre for Poetry in Belfast, Northern Ireland. She has published poetry and essays in New Zealand, Ireland and the UK, and her poetry was recently shortlisted for the 2012 Bridport Poetry Prize (UK).

Magnolia Wilson is from a valley called Fern Flat in the Far North of NZ. She is currently lives in Wellington where she is doing her MA in Creative Writing at Victoria University. She is aware of the stigma attached to MFA programs and thinks it's bullsh%^t. She likes dream-catchers, crystals, and 1970s Ford Escorts.

Alex Taylor is a freelance composer, musician and poet. He was the 2012 NZSO-National Youth Orchestra Composer-in-Residence and the winner of the 2012 SOUNZ Contemporary Award. His poetry is concerned with sonic adventure, the fickleness of emotion, and the relationship between inner (personal) and outer (social) spheres. Alex is a regular performer at the University of Auckland's LOUNGE poetry readings and his work has been published in *Potroast* and *JAAM*.

Lauren Strain lives in Auckland. She likes seconds.

Oliver Quincy Page is a screenwriter, film maker and poet. He hopes to die valiantly saving the Vienna Boy's Choir from the wreckage of a burning tour bus somewhere in the mountains of Tripoli.

MINARETSJOURNAL.COM

www.ingramcontent.com/pod-product-compliance
Lightning Source LLC
Chambersburg PA
CBHW032030040426
42448CB00006B/802